AF339079

# Beauty
## *out of*
# Ashes

# Beauty
## *out of*
# Ashes

AVIN LEE MUI CHOO

**CREATION
HOUSE**

FLOWER PENTECOSTAL
HERITAGE CENTER

Beauty Out Of Ashes
by Avin Lee Mui Choo
Published by Creation House
A Charisma Media Company
600 Rinehart Road
Lake Mary, Florida 32746
www.charismamedia.com

This book or parts thereof may not be reproduced in any form, stored in a retrieval system, or transmitted in any form by any means—electronic, mechanical, photocopy, recording, or otherwise—without prior written permission of the publisher, except as provided by United States of America copyright law.

Unless otherwise noted, all Scripture quotations are from the New King James Version of the Bible. Copyright © 1979, 1980, 1982 by Thomas Nelson, Inc., publishers. Used by permission.

Scripture quotations marked NIV are from the Holy Bible, New International Version of the Bible. Copyright © 1973, 1978, 1984, International Bible Society. Used by permission.

Design Director: Bill Johnson
Cover design by Terry Clifton

Copyright © 2012 by Avin Lee Mui Choo
All rights reserved.

Visit the author's website: www.avinlee.blogspot.com

Library of Congress Cataloging in Publication Data: 2012937898
International Standard Book Number: 978-1-61638-992-5
E-book International Standard Book Number: 978-1-61638-993-2

While the author has made every effort to provide accurate telephone numbers and Internet addresses at the time of publication, neither the publisher nor the author assumes any responsibility for errors or for changes that occur after publication.

First edition

12 13 14 15 16 — 9 8 7 6 5 4 3 2 1
Printed in the United States of America

# ACKNOWLEDGMENTS

FIRSTLY, I WOULD like to acknowledge my dear family: my loving hubby, Heng, and my precious son, Joshua. Heng has been a great support and help throughout the process of writing this book, from its conception to the completion. Joshua has been a source of inspiration to my writing.

Secondly, I want to acknowledge Rev. Kenneth E. Hagin, for his relentless teachings about faith, for it was his books that started me on this faith journey.

Thirdly, I want to acknowledge Pastor Joseph Prince and New Creation Church, especially to Pastor Prince for his teachings on grace (unmerited favor) and in revealing the beauty and goodness of Jesus Christ. It was a personal encounter with my gracious Savior that revolutionized my life.

I also want to acknowledge the editorial and production team at Creation House for their patience and guidance through the entire process of publishing my first book.

Last but not least, I give thanks to Jesus Christ, for it was He who showed me supernatural favor and opened the door for my first book to be published. He deserves all the glory and praise for He is the One who made it all possible! All glory to Jesus!

# TABLE OF CONTENTS

# INTRODUCTION

IT ALL STARTED from a simple idea. One day as I was looking at the journals I kept over the years, I thought about how such journals usually become so precious after the person has passed on. Journals document the life events, thought processes, and experiences of that person. They are an insight to a person's inner life. That's why I have kept the habit of journaling my personal walk with God over the past decade. Even though I am still young, I do not wish that my journals would be put to good use only after I leave. Hence, God put an idea into my mind about writing a book so that I could share my experiences and insights about my own walk with God from my journals. Basically the core message of my book would be on the pure goodness of God. It would talk about how we as children of the Most High God are entitled to all the blessings of this righteousness based on the perfect sacrifice of our Lord, Jesus Christ.

## My Background

I come from a traditional Presbyterian church. It was the first church that I was introduced to that I felt comfortable with back in 1996. At that time I had backslid since I accepted Christ in 1988. I was on the verge of ending a stormy relationship with a non-believer. After my breakup, God brought to my paths caring Christian friends who stood by me during my dark period, and one of them even brought me to her church. I was in that church for thirteen years. In those years, I never once thought about visiting other churches because I felt this was the church that God had planted me in. It is true that God planted me in that church, but only for a season of my life.

I remembered how I felt like fish out of water in that church. I believed God to send a revival because although the church grew, the congregation size had not increased exponentially for about fifty years. I thought that surely over the years, even through the natural multiplication of the families, the numbers must have grown by leaps and bounds! But my pastor was telling me that it was not the size of the congregation that mattered; what mattered more was that there was proper follow-up to the new believers. Some of the megachurches had many new converts but some failed to provide proper follow-up. I accepted his reasoning as I thought it was equally important to focus on discipleship.

In any case, I still hoped to see a revival and I remembered praying to God, "Please do not let me pass on from this world without seeing a revival in this church." That was my heart's desire. Then as the years passed, God put both my husband and I in leadership positions in the church and we saw things more clearly. I really could not put a finger on the core issue, but I felt that we were doing so many things, yet the results did not seem to be forthcoming. Yes, God was still blessing our church, but I somewhat felt it was not the full measure. Then at one point, I felt like there was a form of godliness in the church but lacking its true power.

Although we had many teachings and Bible studies on various books like Romans, Acts, Ephesians, Nehemiah, and so on, I always felt that I could not fully comprehend what was being taught. It was like a veil was put over my heart. The situation was worse when I had to conduct Bible study to my cell group members. I felt like I was the blind leading the blind. I loved this church, and with all due respect to the church, I was not saying that the teachings were ineffective. Maybe it was just me who could not benefit from the teachings. I was not aware that I did not have a firm foundation of Christianity, and it affected the way I responded during a crisis.

## TRIAL AT HOME

In 2003 and 2004 when we had to go through tough times, our faith in God was badly hit. This happened in 2003 when our family went through a crisis, and I hoped that God would have mercy on my brother (who was also a believer) and lighten his punishment. But I could not have asked God for favor because I did not know my standing with God at that time. I thought since this was what my brother deserved, the best I could intercede for on his behalf was a lighter sentence.

---

I was taught that God is merciful but we have to bear the consequences of our mistakes.

---

This was true to a certain extent, but I did not have a revelation of what Christ has done for us at the Cross, and how God would bail us out even if the mistake was of our own making. I did not know how good God was. In my heart, there was a reverent fear of God, knowing that He cannot be arm-twisted. Yet on the other hand, I was secretly hoping that God would acquit my brother. When the verdict finally came out after a grueling six-month period of waiting, the result was devastating to me. What I had believed God for (that my brother would be acquitted) did not materialize. My family was equally shocked, but God is good. What the devil did to destroy, God turned around for our good. Eventually my mum and even my dad came to know Christ.

However, this incident caused a rift in my trust for God. I started to wonder whether God was really that good. If He was, then why did He not intervene to save my brother from that situation? I had no answer to that painful question in my heart. But one day, God showed me something else. He showed me the Cross. He showed me the scene when Jesus cried, *"Eli, Eli, lama sabachthani?"* that is, "My God, My God, why have You forsaken Me?" (Matt. 27:46). At that time, I did not have full revelation of what God was trying to tell me. But the greatest comfort I had was that Jesus knew the pain and the heartache I went through, as He had experienced the worst kind of pain on the cross, and He fully understood. That to me was sufficient for an answer at that time.

Little did I know that I had not fully gotten over the incident. I had not resolved the fundamental issue in my heart about the goodness of God. This was so crucial because that is the basis of our faith in God. How can we be sure we have the answer we asked God for if we are not fully convinced that we serve a good God?

## Trial in Pregnancy

And so, the second attack came soon after my brother's incident. This time it was about my own flesh. We had been trying for a baby since 2002, before my brother's incident. It was frustrating enough to not have success in baby making, what more to handle the level of stress from my brother's case. The case finally concluded in mid 2003, and I found myself pregnant in early 2004. It was a peculiar pregnancy because the pregnancy tests were vaguely positive. As a result, I did not dare to rejoice over it, though it had been our hearts' desires all this while.

When we went for a first scan, the doctor could not see the pregnancy sac clearly but he said it might be too early. Then I started bleeding and was admitted to the hospital. I had to be bedridden. The doctor still could not find the sac and suggested for me to go for a laparoscopy to rule out the possibility of an ectopic pregnancy. The baby was not found in my fallopian tubes but the doctor still could not see the baby in my womb. The whole painful incident ended with menstruation, which actually was a relief for me because I could not imagine being bedridden for the entire pregnancy period.

During the period of waiting for the pregnancy to stabilize, I was actually in fear. I was saying words of fear rather than faith.

---

Even though I quoted scriptures,
I did not know I was saying
them out of fear, not faith.

---

Of course there were more doubts than before regarding why God had allowed this to happen to me. It certainly did not help that the previous doubts lingering from my brother's incident compounded the issue.

After the miscarriage, I was devastated. I really did not know how to go to God or whether He would even answer my prayers. My faith was badly hit. I kept crying and crying over the loss of my baby. But in my heart, I knew it was something worse. It was the entire loss of faith in God. My relationship with God was at stake. I slipped into depression. During that period, God spoke to me about His love for me, how He loved me before I was born and when I was growing up. Knowing His love for me did comfort my soul for a while.

But the turning point came when I began to have suicidal thoughts…it was so bad that my husband was afraid to leave me alone even for a while. I remembered the time he cried, telling me, "Please don't be so selfish to end your life. You know it hurts me so much to see you like this. I love you so much, please don't leave me behind." At that point I woke up from my depression. I thought to myself, I really should not be so selfish. I still have a hubby who loves me so much. I still have a God who loves me so much.

**Chapter 1**

# MY JOURNEY WITH
# FAITH TEACHINGS

IF YOU ASKED me if I ever thought about giving up on God, I would say I did. But I knew in my heart, if I held on to Jesus, He would restore everything back to me one day. If I gave up Jesus, everything would be really lost. (Years later, I realized that it was not me who hung on to Jesus. It was Jesus who hung on to me all this while. It must have shattered His heart to see me suffer needlessly. His heart was crushed at the Cross. Now it was crushed again.)

## Road to Recovery

Now the road to full recovery was gradual, but God was faithful. He sent believers in our church who had been to RHEMA Bible Training Center Singapore and exposed to faith teachings to minister to us. The amazing thing happened during a holiday trip to Hokkaido in September 2004. God gave a verse to my husband. It was Mark 11:23–24 when Jesus told His disciples, "For assuredly, I say to you, whoever says to this mountain, 'Be removed and be cast into the sea,' and does not doubt in his heart, but believes that those things he says will be done, he will have whatever he says. Therefore I say to you, whatever things you ask when you pray, believe that you receive them and you will have them."

My husband seldom remembered his dreams, but this time it was very clear to him. We did not know that these verses were the very core teachings of Rev. Kenneth E. Hagin, a great man of faith. Though we had just been introduced to the faith teachings, we took to them very quickly. We were so hungry for God's Word, especially in the area of faith. We devoured every audio CD and book that was lent to us. We also sought out the Christian bookstores on these teachings.

We grew leaps and bounds in our revelation of His Word. Another high point for me was receiving the baptism of the Holy Spirit, which led me to speak in tongues. Wow, that experience was spectacular! I remembered I was praying with the other Spirit-filled believers and

I asked them how to receive this gift of tongues. They started speaking in tongues and then amazingly I found myself speaking in tongues too! Then my elder in my previous church laid his hands on me and I could feel the power of the anointing. I kept falling down, until I was flat on the floor!

That was the open door to even more revelations and the mysteries of God's plan started to unfold in my life. It was like my daily prayer of Ephesians 1:17–18 coming true. Gradually I had the spirit of wisdom and revelation to know Christ better and the eyes of my heart were opened to see the hope of His calling, the riches of His glorious inheritance in the saints, and the surpassing great power for us who believe. Life for me had taken on a whole new meaning because I could now hear God more clearly.

---

The veil slowly began to lift as we learned about the believers' authority in Christ, living the faith-filled life and learning to confess the Word of God in our daily lives.

---

## God's Restoration of a Child

We also learned about restoration and how God would repay us for what the devil has stolen from us. From then on, we were sure that it was God's will for us to have children, even though people around us told us that we were still complete as a family unit without children, or that we could consider adoption. We believed that God had commanded us to be fruitful and multiply and fill the earth. We started searching scriptures on what God said about childbearing and found Exodus 23:25–26: "So you shall serve the Lord your God, and He will bless your bread and your water. And I will take sickness away from the midst of you. No one shall suffer miscarriage or be barren in your land."

We started confessing that we were pregnant and that God had given us this child. And we kept thanking God for this baby even though the manifestation had not yet come. The stronghold of wondering if there was something wrong about us that had caused the miscarriage to happen or had made us wait so long to conceive was destroyed. We believed that our marriage was greatly blessed by God; and instead of being shaken by the crisis, our love grew stronger each day. And God's delays were not His denials. One day He would exalt us with a child and our joy would be so great! He would restore the years the locusts had eaten and we would see how He turned the situation around again, as He has done in the past! We believed we would be more blessed than the rest, than those who already had children!

It was true that right believing led to right living. As our faith grew, our hearts became more ready to receive this child that God had already given. My doubts about the goodness of God were slowly being addressed as I allowed the truths of God's Word to take root in my heart. I really thank God for the revelation given to me in Kenneth E. Hagin's book, *Don't Blame God.*[1] Indeed, God was showing me that He yearned to bless us, not curse us. The curse of sin and the law was borne by Jesus. In exchange for our curse, Christ has given us His blessings! That was the first time I was introduced to the finished work of Christ on the cross, but this teaching was not yet expounded on in detail.

I also learned that the bad things that happened were not from God, but God might allow them to happen, yet turning the outcome into something beautiful! I realized at that point that God was not the author of such things. It was the devil's doing and his lies all along. Another revelation was that God intended us to have a child long, long ago. The child was ours to claim. Hope says, "I will be pregnant sometime." Heart faith says, "The baby belongs to me now." Since God had spoken so clearly and He said His words would not be delayed any longer, we decided to march straight on and claim the baby.

## FULFILLMENT OF GOD'S PROMISE OF A CHILD

God also taught me something very powerful. It was the power of visualization. Matthew 9:29 says, "According to your faith let it be to you." There was one particular month when I felt like I was pregnant and I could almost visualize how easy it was to become pregnant. I could foresee how I would break this good news to my family, my cell members, my sisters, friends, colleagues, and so forth. It was so real…like never before. That feeling was amazing, and I knew God was giving me a taste of how it would be when I was really pregnant, even though I did not conceive that month.

God led me to start praying for this little one using the book, *Praying for Your Unborn Child*[2] even before I confirmed pregnant. In His mercy, He also revealed the nature of this child who would be born to us.

> I learned that when God was about to perform a mighty work, He caused a child to be born. From and through that child came the fulfillment of His mighty purposes.

Besides, I understood that God had a purpose for the wait. Because how I would handle rejection and ridicule, even great sorrow and pain, would create an atmosphere in my home that would have a solid character-building effect on our children, enabling them to have the same qualities in their relationship with God.

He also encouraged me to persevere because the time to conceive was near. He even showed me Matthew 24:32, "When its branch has already become tender and puts forth leaves, you know that summer is near." Verse 33 says, "So you also, when you see all these things, know that it is near—at the doors!" God was telling me to expectantly look out for this pregnancy through a series of events (my team of staff being formed, my office shift, and so forth) that would happen. And indeed it came to pass according to what God told me.

In November 2005, I was finally pregnant with my first baby! No amount of words could describe how grateful I was to God! If you asked me whether the fears of the miscarriage affected me during this pregnancy period, I would say no. I really thank God because this time around, I had filled my heart with faith and my mouth with faith-filled words. There was really no room for fear. Besides, I had a solid assurance that since it was God's will for me to conceive again, He would certainly bring this baby to this world safely. I did not have to worry because nothing that I did or ate would affect my baby's health. God was the One who sustained my pregnancy.

We also confessed that every doctor visit was blessed, and indeed it happened according to what we believed. I remembered how joyful, blessed, and healthy I was during my first pregnancy. I could even work right until the week that I gave birth (which was just two days before my due date). Although I believed God for supernatural childbirth (with no pain and no stitches), my birth was through caesarean. That was because I was induced and in labor for eighteen hours, and by the time my doctor came, I was totally exhausted from waiting. Yet the amazing part was that I did not experience any labor pains when my womb had contractions. Even the nurse was surprised. She said most women would have flipped by then. In any case I thanked God for a smooth, safe, painless, and blessed delivery. When baby Joshua was born in August 2006, our joy as a family was complete.

◆

# Chapter 2

# LIFE AS A MOTHER

For the next ten months, I stayed home taking care of baby Joshua. By God's grace, I was able to take no-pay leave to stay home. It was indeed a blessed period because I could breastfeed my baby. It was a wonderful bonding time with him. I was getting the hang of taking care of a small baby, and the fact that Joshua was an easy baby made it more enjoyable. However, after a while, I got a little bored with staying at home as I craved human interaction. I began to bring Joshua for walks and was very happy if I saw stay-home mums like me. I would eagerly start conversations with them.

But such interactions were not sufficient to "fend

away" my boredom. I was happy to spend the weekends with my husband and Joshua, as we would usually go out. But when Monday came, I was kind of lost, wondering what I would do for the rest of the weekdays. Where could I go? Whom could I visit? There were some stay-home mums in my church but some of them were also busy with taking care of their children. I did meet up with a few of them in my stay-home period, but somehow I felt something missing in my soul.

## Missing Ministry Work

I used to be quite active in ministry, serving in cell group and prayer ministry before I became a mother. Though having kids was my heart's desire, the reality was that I still had to adjust to motherhood. I knew I had to change my role from frontline ministry to home ministry (where I took care of my son, Joshua), while my husband took on a leadership position in the church. I must say it was not that easy, especially when my baby was small. Motherhood was a 24/7 vocation, as in there was no time off like how you could take leave from work. It was a continuous task and very intensive, as your baby needs your full attention. It could be disruptive in a sense that you could not even have a proper conversation with another sister in church on Sunday. Mothers, you know what I mean.

Sometimes when I was caught up with the mundane tasks of motherhood, I lost perspective of my calling and my role in the process. I remembered feeling rather jealous that my husband could continue to serve in church while I had to take care of Joshua and wait for him to finish his meetings. I had become weary, tired, and restless, like Martha. What was worse was that I could not even have a healthy intake of God's Word on Sunday, as my time was spent chasing after my toddler in nursery (back then in my church). When I was under-nourished, how then could I pour out God's love into my son?

## The Truth About Healing

It was enjoyable taking care of baby Joshua until he reached six months old. That was when Joshua started to have fever, diarrhea, infection, runny nose, cough, and other symptoms. Then once it started, it just kept recurring. Many times I prayed for his healing. I knew it was God's will to heal him, but sometimes the healing did not manifest soon enough. Twice I fell sick taking care of him. It seemed like a never-ending cycle. I felt so tired and began to wonder if I was suitable to stay home to take care of Joshua in the long run.

I thought that going back to work might be a better option. At least I could have a more balanced life. It was enjoyable to take care of him when he was healthy, but when he was sick, it was really trying! Oh how I hated the diseases that kept harassing my baby! I told God, "Since You created Joshua, I am sure You know how to maintain his perfect health!" I was tired because I had been using my own strength. I thought it might be better if I did not have to face Joshua all the time. Then I would not get so affected by these ailments.

Parents in my church who meant well tried to comfort me that these childhood sicknesses were part and parcel of growing up. I refused to accept this reasoning.

---

I did not know whether accepting such sicknesses would make it easier for me to handle them. What I knew was that such sicknesses were certainly not God's will for us.

---

We are God's covenant people. We have the Holy Spirit, we have the anointing; we have God's power within us. How can we live so pathetically? At that time, I literally cried out to the Lord on behalf of my child!

I told God that He must have loved Joshua more than I did. Hence I wanted to entrust Joshua into God's hands. I implored the Lord to show me if it was His will for me to accept all these sicknesses and still be contented and joyful about it. If it were so, I would not ask Him about the healing anointing anymore! I would take it that this was just not meant for us. We would just live our lives as before, pretending that we never knew about this healing anointing.

Deep down in my heart, I knew the anointing was for me but I did not know how to appropriate God's power. I knew I needed to have faith, and faith comes from hearing God's Word. One day, I found God's Word in Exodus 23:25: "So you shall serve the LORD your God and He will bless your bread and your water. And I will take sickness away from the midst of you."

At this confirmation of His Word, I greatly rejoiced because God was telling me that I could operate at a higher level of faith than the healing anointing. I could stand on God's Word that sicknesses would not even come near us! At that time even though Joshua was still having a runny or stuffy nose, I chose to believe that he was healed. And after this time, there would be no more sickness in his body because we stood on God's Word.

To tell the truth, it was really not easy to have faith in God's Word as I was looking at the natural situation. I still got affected each time as Joshua cried when he was disturbed by his stuffy nose. But faith was the key to releasing God's healing power. And I needed to have faith to activate the power. I sensed that my faith was being stretched to another level. It was tough but I knew that I was moving in the right direction. That was why I was facing so many obstacles that I almost wanted to give up searching for the truth.

## RETURN TO THE WORKFORCE

When my no-pay leave came to an end, I had very mixed feelings. On one hand, I felt reluctant to leave Joshua to go back to work. In fact, I cried twice regarding this issue, asking God to reveal whether it was His will for me to go back to work. I had other stay-home mothers in my church telling me that it would be such a shame if I could not continue taking care of my baby, because he would be small only once. I did not want to lose the chance to see my baby growing up; but on the other hand, I looked forward to working, because only when I went back to work would my self-identity return. Otherwise, through staying at home, my identity would be intertwined with Joshua's.

I am always a mother, and that role was not only intense, it was overwhelming. I enjoyed staying at home with Joshua but I needed a balance. I felt I needed the social and mental interaction. I needed to talk to people, to joke and to be playful. Sometimes I thank God I had a job to go back to. I was quite sure it was God's will for me to return to work in this season of my life. I felt that having too much of a good thing (taking care of baby) might turn out to be suboptimal.

Hence at that point in time, I knew God had plans to prosper me, to give me a hope and a future in my workplace. He wanted to bless me richly and make me a blessing to others. He wanted to make use of my abilities to glorify Him and He wanted me to find great satisfaction in my work. Therefore I was very convinced that God would take care of the transition. Joshua and I would adjust very well. As it turned out, it was indeed a joyful transition as I was able to telecommute two days a week to ease into the transition.

I started work for three months and though work had been quite fulfilling, it was tiring. I realized that sometimes I let the work stress affect me. It manifested in dreams and restless sleep, especially during the busy periods. Working from home helped but because it was not official (a special favor granted by my Director), I sometimes felt uncomfortable when people asked if I was in the office. But I got over this because I knew it was God's will. In any case, I still did my work and delivered my projects on time. I thank God that I had an understanding boss and good staff to cover me.

Before I became a mother, I used to take leave to come home and rest, spending time with God. But during those months, I was not able to spend time alone with God due to the busyness.

---

Time alone with God was such a luxurious thing for a mother. Somehow having a baby numbed a mother to her needs.

---

Many times, it is amazing how tired mothers can carry on endlessly, though I know it is not healthy. God did not make us that way. I thank God that He made me a reflective person. There were alarm bells in my life when I knew I needed to seek God. When I was tired or drained or impatient or critical, I knew something was not right. Yet I felt I needed to run to God more regularly. I prayed for daily times of refreshing with Him. I knew He would meet me at my level of need.

# God's Plan for Mothers

The more I sought God, the more I saw His goodness and His love. I learned that God loves us mothers very much and wanted us to celebrate our lives as beautiful individuals with our divine destinies. We were, after all, still individuals with needs, and He wanted to meet those needs. It could be the need to still look good, to be involved in ministries, to have a healthy intake of God's Word or maybe just to have a good rest at the feet of Jesus.

Our identity was separate from our kids. God saw us as glorious looking, not troublesome or nagging mothers. He saw us with great worth because we are children of the Most High God. I used to think that God was done with my life and my ministry after I became a mother, but I was challenged with this thought: God was going to bring me to greater heights than I had soared before. He still had a way to bring those latent dreams and desires in my heart to come to pass. He was not finished with my life yet. *My best life has yet to come.*

In April 2008, God gave me an idea of starting a mothers' fellowship in my old church—a time for the young mothers to share, pray, and encourage one another with God's Word, without the distraction of the kids. I reckoned that as a mother of one child then, if I was struggling, then the rest of the mothers must have been struggling more with more children. Some mothers had even "resigned" themselves to the fact that this was just a phase they needed to endure when their kids were small.

Although this idea did not materialize at that time, the seed was already planted in my heart. I knew my ministry was to reach out to the mothers. This ministry would be a great blessing because it was birthed out of God's heartbeat for the mothers. He wanted us to see ourselves with a strategic role: raising champion kids, "movers and shakers," and leaders of God in the next generation. He wanted us to leave a legacy in our children's lives that would impact even future generations. He intended for us to play a part in the fulfillment of our children's divine destinies while He was also working on our divine destinies.

◆

# Chapter 3

# CALLING OUT OF MY OLD CHURCH

IN EARLY 2008, I came to a point that I was totally dissatisfied with my life. I did not feel fulfilled at work, in church, or in my personal life. I knew God had called me to be a happy mother of children at home yet it was not time for me to quit my job to stay home full-time. On the other hand, I was not enjoying my work because nothing in my organization seemed to move. I felt that I was just clocking time and not making any contribution to my job. I remember asking God what was His will in this season of my life, but He said, "Can I not show you? I want you to trust Me. This is a faith test." And He gave me this verse: "Be still and know that I am God" (Ps. 46:10).

In church, I was not fulfilled because I was lacking in the intake of the Word while taking care of Joshua in the nursery. I was tired and really questioned the value of coming to church. In my personal life, I was not seeing any progress or results from our efforts of trying for our second baby. I knew God wanted to give us this child but the manifestation seemed far away. This was a trying time in my life when I really felt dry spiritually. Everything in my life seemed to come to a standstill. Nothing was moving. I felt like I was in the wilderness.

## Trials in Parenting

Then the trials seemed to invade my life, when my heart was troubled. First it was Joshua's viral infection that landed him in hospital with bronchitis. The next few months I was so worried that he would have another bout of bronchitis every time he had a cough. It was a terrible period of fear and unrest because I was so concerned about his lungs being adversely affected by the bronchitis. Somehow I totally forgot about the revelation in Exodus 23:25 that God will take away sickness from us. I had let go of the Word of God. It was really trying because after Joshua got well, I fell sick. And each time I fell sick, I got even more frustrated because it would affect our trying for a second baby. And if I did not conceive and give birth to another child, how I could leave this unfulfilling workplace? It was really a downward spiral.

The last straw came around the period when we were

intending to put Joshua in a playgroup. I was trying my best to look for one that was near to my mum's place and a place that was comfortable for Joshua. At that time, I was kind of driven by fear again. It was a fear of Joshua's seemingly slow speech development. You see, after he recovered from those months of sickness, he had somewhat become withdrawn and quiet. Sometimes he was even moody. He took to watching TV and seemed disinterested in talking or communicating with people. It really pained my heart to see him like this because he was born a cheerful and responsive baby. So I thought the solution was to send him to a playgroup so that he could interact with other toddlers and learn to talk.

I enrolled him in a playgroup near my mum's place but Joshua was still not settling well, even after a few times there. If he found out that we had left, he would cry non-stop until the playgroup was over. I had to take leave to settle him into the playgroup and I was really frustrated that he could not overcome his separation anxiety. I eventually had to pull him out of the class because he was not settling in well. My husband and I decided to wait till he was older before putting him into childcare.

## START OF RIPPLES

At the same time, things at work started changing. My most valued staff member, the one on whom I depended a lot for my department's work, announced to me that she was leaving. Someone had poached her to join their team and after much consideration, she decided that she should leave. She was also reluctant to leave and she had tears in her eyes as she told me her difficult decision. However, she knew she needed to go because it was God's will for her. I really felt that my comfort zone was totally being invaded. I knew things would be very different when she left. It did not help that I was also very tired of my work and already thought of leaving.

I was so desperate to leave that I asked God for an open door. I thought perhaps I could take on part-time work in one of the polytechnics. This idea came after my sister-in-law gave birth and my brother had intended for my mum to take care of his baby. They were thinking of getting a maid and asked me to share the cost since my mum would be taking care of two small children and would definitely need help. My husband and I were totally uncomfortable with the thought of a maid taking care of Joshua. We thought, rather than a maid taking care of our son, why don't I take care of him myself? After all, it was my heart's desire to spend more time with my son.

God actually showed me an open door. The interview at the polytechnic went smoothly and I got the job. I was just waiting for the administrative procedures to go through. However, I did not really feel the peace in my heart. I thought if two of us left the team, what would happen to my boss? Who would support him? I really did not want to be irresponsible and leave at this time, especially when my boss has shown such favor to me all along. Besides, the government had just announced that there would be four months of maternity leave from the next year onward, and I would be giving up my year-end bonus, which would be a waste.

Hence I decided that I would not leave unless I had the peace. I felt that it was not time for me to leave my company yet—like I had unfinished business here. But I told God, "You need to do three things for me if it is Your will for me to stay. Firstly, You need to let me find favor in the course of my work. Secondly, You need to bless the work of my hands and make my projects move. Thirdly, You need to send another good team member to replace the one that just left." Of course, God answered all my prayers. He is so good.

## STIRRINGS IN OUR HEARTS

On the church front, things also started to move. We were introduced to Pastor Joseph Prince's teachings by an elder in our church in the early part of 2008. When we started hearing this gospel of grace, something in our hearts stirred. It was an excitement that we could not explain and we could not contain. We were addicted to his teachings. We wanted more. Hence I kept praying to God asking Him to open a door for us to visit New Creation Church (NCC), since we did not know anyone there.

In October 2008, God showed me Hebrews 12:26, "Yet once more I shake not only the earth, but also heaven," and Ezekiel 12:28, "None of My words will be postponed any more, but the word which I speak will be done." I sensed that God was shifting my season and there was a shaking going on in my work, my church, and my personal life.

> I then realized that all God was doing previously was part of His plan—He was shaking things up, pulling us out of our comfort zone and realigning things.

And though I did not like it, as it was uncomfortable on the backside of the desert, I know it was necessary to prepare us for the path ahead.

God worked miraculously—He led me to talk to my auntie during one of the family gatherings and I realized that not only was she attending NCC, but also my uncle (who used to be against Christianity) had accepted Christ and they were both attending church! What a great testimony! My auntie said she could help us queue up for service and reserve seats for us! God really knew my heart's desires!

We stepped into NCC in November 2008, and from the first service we attended, we knew our lives would be different. It was like the church resonated with all of our being, from the worship, to the Holy Communion, to the sermon by Pastor Joseph Prince. We left service that day feeling even hungrier for God's Word. It seemed like we could not get enough of Jesus and His finished work on the cross in our old church's sermon. Yes, Christ was preached during the sermons, but not in the paramount way like NCC.

---

In New Creation Church, everything
revolved around Jesus, unveiling
His beauty and perfection in the
Old and New Testaments.

---

The gospel of grace revolutionized our life in such a way that nothing remained the same. For me, it was the first time after so long I felt alive spiritually. Not only that, everything seemed to be moving faster than before (in my work, my church, and my personal life). I became more fulfilled as I was slowly being filled with the Word every day.

## KEY DIFFERENCES IN THE MESSAGES

Ever since we attended NCC, I had been learning all about the gospel of grace and understanding why this gospel had been under fire. Hence I just wanted to highlight the key differences between this gospel of grace and the gospel that I had been exposed to since I became a believer.

### Gospel of Grace

Focus on the finished work of Christ. A divine exchange has taken place at the Cross. What Christ has suffered (heartache, pain, sicknesses, poverty, condemnation, etc.) we need not suffer again.

Because Jesus cried, "My God, My God, why have You forsaken Me?" we can now say, "My Father, my Father, why have You so blessed me?"

We are now under a new covenant of grace; the old covenant of law has been replaced. We now enjoy unmerited favor from God.

We have confidence that His blessings are based on Christ's finished work, not our own performance. We are blessed to be a blessing to the world.

There was one perfect sacrifice at the cross for all our sins: past, present, and future. With Christ's perfect sacrifice on the cross, God has promised that He will remember our sins and lawless deeds no more (Heb. 8:12).

We need not fear His fiery judgment because it was all poured out on Jesus. God does not want us to be sin-conscious but righteousness-conscious. When we know the heavy price Christ paid for our right standing, we will not see this grace as a license to sin.

Righteousness is a gift just like salvation. We only need to believe that Christ came to give us righteousness; it is not something we can earn. We cannot be more righteous by our works.

Right believing always leads to right living. We are already holy and accepted in God's eyes because of Christ.

We are God's beloved children and we have an inheritance in Christ. He wants us to be firmly established in righteousness.

## Mixed Teachings of Law and Grace

What Christ has done has bought us eternal salvation but sometimes we still need to go the way of the Cross. We need to take up our cross and partake in the fellowship of the sufferings of Christ.

I never heard about the new covenant of grace hence I was in fear of God's judgment in the Old Testament.

Sometimes I felt that the blessings of God are dependent on my actions like those Israelites under the old covenant.

I was taught that we are channels of God's blessings but I felt the focus was on what we should do to be a blessing, rather than on the finished work of Christ.

I was taught that when we sin, we need to confess our sins to God (1 John 1:9). This implied that the blood of Jesus could only cover our sins till the next one.

Our relationship with God is not broken but our fellowship can by broken by our sin. Hence we need to confess our sins and repent, so that our fellowship with God will be re-established and He will hear our prayers. Sometimes God seems far and distant when in fact, He is always near.

We got to be more holy by the pursuit of spiritual disciplines like quiet time with God, praying, fasting, etc.

There is still some part for us to perform after being saved. Some books even teach that salvation could be lost. That will not give believers security if their faith is based on themselves. Besides, that would not give us confidence to come to the throne of grace in times of need.

## Time to Move!

We were hooked on to Pastor Prince's teachings and in just a few months, my husband told me we needed to make a decision. We were straddling two churches then and we knew it was not healthy. We could only belong to one church and we could not be listening to mixed messages from both churches. It was like new wine cannot be poured into old wineskins or else both would be destroyed (Luke 5:37).

> I still remembered sitting on the pews of my old church one Sunday listening to the sermon and God told me, "Find out more about the finished work of Christ on the cross."

My pastor was not even preaching on the topic of the finished work! It was amazing how God spoke to me so clearly.

It was not a rash decision because we had given it much thought and deliberation. We were leaving our comfort zone, leaving a church we attended for thirteen years and the long-time friends in our cell group. Of course we could not bear to leave our brothers and sisters in the cell group. After all, we had walked together through the years. We sought God's will and He gave us this verse in Isaiah 55:12, "You shall go out with joy, and be led out with peace." He was prophesying the manner in which we would leave this church. This was very important to us because we had seen so much bitterness in which members left church. We wanted to leave without stumbling anyone especially when my husband was a leader at that time.

We felt we were like Abraham in Genesis 12:1. God called Abraham out of Ur in order to bless him so that he would be a blessing to the nations. We wanted the blessings of God on our lives and we wanted to be a blessing. So when God said, "Time to move!" it was decision time very quickly. We had to adjust our lives so that we could go with God; otherwise we would miss His divine shifts and what He wanted to accomplish in our lives, which was more important.

Hence we made the difficult decision to leave everything in our church and move on to NCC. Making the decision was tough enough but announcing the decision, especially to our pastor and cell members was even more difficult. It was an emotional and sentimental scene but I told myself after that I must move on. I must cut the sentimental ties, forget the past and move forward to the calling God has for our family.

God is really so good. He gave us more than what we expected. In the last prayer meeting that my husband led, a group of elders and deacons called our family out, and prayed a prayer of blessing over us before sending us out of this church. There were tears but they knew it was God's will for us and they had to let us go. Indeed, God fulfilled His promise of leading us out in peace and joy. With that, we closed the chapter in our old church and began our new life in NCC. That was when our lives got more exciting.

**Chapter 4**

# CALLING OUT OF MY OLD WORKPLACE

SHORTLY AFTER WE crossed over completely to NCC, things also started shaking in my workplace. Firstly we received news that our office would be moving back from its current location to the headquarters by the end of 2009. This was the beginning of the ripples, though I still was not sure what was coming up. We had been in this office for almost four years and it held many fond memories. With this impending move, I had a sense that my season on the work front had shifted and the time of waiting was coming to an end.

## SHAKING IN THE WORKPLACE

Around the same time we heard about our change of CEO effective from August 2009. It was truly amazing how fast things moved because we did not expect our current CEO to be changed, since we knew he was retiring in two years' time. With this change in leadership, my organization was also entering into a new season; but like my old church, I felt that I also had no role to play in this new season. However, I knew I needed to stay on for a little while more.

The news of the change in leadership was exciting but at the same time frightening. I was reminded of the change in leadership in my previous workplace and the re-organization in 2004. The devil brought to my mind how I was condemned in the previous re-organization and how I left the company in total defeat. I got into unrest but yet I knew God had a wonderful plan of restoration for me this time round.

> I was reminded that this restoration was already a finished work in God's eyes. It was not dependent on my actions, but on what I believed.

All I had to do was cooperate with Him and act when He instructed me. Even though I wanted badly to get pregnant then, I knew that my focus should be on closing this chapter well. Besides, things started to get exciting at work with our new CEO, and hence this took my mind off my pregnancy issue for a while.

God gave a vision of me leaving my organization with my head lifted high and a promise of how I would leave this place in joy and peace (Isa. 55:12), like how we left our old church. God told me that the battle belonged to Him and all I had to do was stand still and see the victory!

Around that time I also found out that in the re-organization, my Director (my boss, who brought me into this organization) was no longer my supervisor. I felt rather sentimental about it but I knew things like this happen during change of leadership. It was made worse when my new CEO shared about his vision of the new place that we were moving to (not the headquarters), and I totally could not see myself in his vision. I was sure that God was calling me out of that place, except that I still did not know when to leave.

In the subsequent months, there were so many times I felt overwhelmed and burnt out because of the many changes in my workplace: my new supervisor and my new portfolio. I was discouraged because I had relied on my strength (self-efforts) and not rested upon God's grace.

We moved back to headquarters from our current location in November 2009 on the same day that happened to be my Director's last day in this organization. He was moving on to another workplace. I was really sentimental about it because I'd had the time of my life in that office, but God encouraged me that my time in this organization was really coming to an end as well. God also told me He would show me a glimpse of my future ministry (which He revealed to another sister), and He reminded me that after this shaking, the glory of the latter house would be greater than the former (Hag. 2:9).

By the end of 2009, I was feeling weary again and I was out of steam. I really did not know how I was going to face the New Year. I felt that I had waited a long time for His promise of another child and of staying home. I began to wonder if His promise was really coming to pass, or whether I had even heard Him correctly in the first place. Yet in my heart, I knew that this workplace was a transitional one; but the wait was much longer than I expected. I even wondered if the delay of another child was due to God's preparation of my change in vocation (i.e. to stay home); and if so, I was willing to compromise His plan for the immediate fulfillment of this promise. I felt that I really could not wait any longer.

## God's Restoration in the Workplace

God is so good. He never fails to encourage me with His Word. I came across Pastor Joel Osteen's book, *It's Your Time*[1], and it so ministered to me. I felt that God was speaking to me plainly and clearly, addressing all my worries and concerns. It was a word from God in season so that I could have the strength to carry on. God kept telling me that my time was here and I was next in line to receive His promise (of staying home).

At that time I also realized that 2010 would be the seventh year of restoration (from my defeated exit from my previous company in 2004). I started to get excited all over again, for I knew that this time around, God would surely bring me out of this place victoriously! Somehow I sensed that God wanted to restore the glory and honor that I lost in the previous re-organization.

In early 2010, God told me He would restore double in this re-organization and that He would lead me out before the organization's move to the new place. He also assured me of His provision for the next three years while I stayed home. In Leviticus 25:21, the Scriptures said, "Then I will command My blessing on you in the sixth year, and it will bring forth produce enough for three years." God also gave me a vision of a condominium community with other stay-home mums and showed me what I would be doing at home (taking care of my children, cooking dinner, and so forth).

I was convinced that the season has shifted and God confirmed His will for me in my next season: to be a happy mother of children at home (Ps. 113:9). I also knew that when all this came to pass, I would have an even more impactful testimony about my second pregnancy that would bring glory to God. It would be a supernatural pregnancy and a miracle ahead. At the end of 2010, we would see that we were ten times more blessed than other people. Even though the first few months of 2010 were tough and I wanted to quit my job many times, it was this promise of God that kept me going on.

Little did I know that God was working out something marvelous behind the scenes; while I was agonizing over why God was delaying my exit from this increasingly intolerable workplace, God was putting me at the right place and the right time. Our team was working on a proposal that would bring continual government funding for degree courses in the arts institutions.

This was something that previous teams had worked on for the past ten years but there was no apparent breakthrough. However, now the timing was right and we had the backing from another government body, hence things fell into place quickly and we got the funding approval. I could say that the success in obtaining the funding was the biggest achievement I had in this workplace and the legacy that I could leave behind. Yet this was nothing that I could boast about because it was all God's work, not mine. As He had mentioned to me earlier, all I had to do was cooperate with Him.

The completion of this proposal was part of His restoration plan.

> It was necessary for me to witness this marvelous work that God had graciously included me in, in order that I might know that with Christ, all things are possible.

It was important because for the many years I had spent in this organization, I never really had a sense of job satisfaction, which in turn adversely affected my self-esteem.

Although it was not about works or self-efforts, God showed me that with Him by my side guiding me, He was able to cause me to do great things. I learned what He meant by this: "I can do all things through Christ who strengthens me" (Phil. 4:13). In doing so, He also answered my earlier prayer request to leave this workplace with a legacy. God is really so good. He remembered my request even though I had forgotten about it.

## Confusion Sets In

In mid 2010, however, I did not know how but I got all confused again. Because I could not wait for the new season to commence, I started to convince myself that maybe my next season had already started. The new season was in this workplace. I thought that maybe God wanted me to stay in this place for a couple more years, like coming back here after giving birth to my second child. It was quite absurd considering that God had told me so clearly in the beginning of the year that my next season was to be a stay-home mum. Yet at that time, I was reaching my limits, and the only way to remain sane while waiting was to tell myself that the waiting had ended and my new season had begun.

God was so merciful. He quickly pulled me out of my workplace for three weeks to speak to me. In those wonderful times of fellowship with Him, God showed me once again that my role in this company was coming to an end. God was accelerating things so that I could leave soon. Then I realized the intense feelings I had were the beginning of labor pangs or contractions. I was close to giving birth to my dreams. I was at the threshold and it was always the most difficult just before birth. In those three weeks, God gave more clarity about my future ministry: writing, counseling, and ministering to mothers, among other things.

At the end of my three-week leave, I sensed that I had finally given birth to my dreams: my second child and my writing ministry. God told me to rejoice and celebrate because the births were spectacular. These victories were not mundane. God also gave me a mandate: Get ready to move on now. Because of God's Word, I felt like I had received the second wind to give the final push, to finish the last lap.

When I went back to work in July 2010, I was no longer confused or discouraged. I knew that what God said would happen very soon, although I did not know how or when. I still harbored hopes that I would get pregnant soon, give birth, and then leave this workplace. But God had other plans. He was accelerating things and they would happen sooner than I thought.

## PURCHASE OF OUR NEW HOME

True enough, things began moving much faster after God gave His mandate. We had been looking for a second property since the previous year, but our finances were insufficient for the down payment. But somehow in July 2010, God prompted my husband to start looking for this private property. Hence we went to look at some condominium units in a few places. There was this particular condo that my husband had been eyeballing for a few years. I was not so keen because this place was a bit out of the way and not close to any Mass Rapid Transit (MRT) stations. In response, my husband said that there was a condo shuttle service to the nearest MRT station.

In any case, he convinced me to at least take a look at the units in this development. When our family first stepped into this place, I instinctively knew that this was the place that God had given us for our new home. I felt so tranquil and relaxed in this place. I could almost see our family living here. Even my son, Joshua, liked this place very much because of the landscaping and the swimming pools. We went to look at a few units and there was one particular unit that we really liked.

However, we felt that we could not afford the price that the seller was looking for. We might not have enough cash to pay the down payment since we were not selling our Housing Development Board (HDB) flat. I thought we might need to borrow cash for the down payment, but God clearly told me, "You shall lend to many nations, but you shall not borrow" (Deut. 28:12). To cut the long story short, God provided the cash in the form of our Central Provident Fund (CPF) savings. We found out that we could use a portion of our CPF to pay the down payment. And so we bought our dream home in August 2010! Praise Jesus!

With that purchase of our second property, we could rent out our fully paid-up HDB flat and enjoy a good rental income every month. I realized that the vision God had given me in the beginning of the year was really coming to pass! Not only that, God had provided our family with this rental income so that I could stay home in style and my husband would not be burdened financially. God is really so good. His provision was exceedingly more than what we asked or imagined!

---

## Besides, the purchase of this private property was a symbol of God's promise to bless us financially.

---

The reality that God was prospering us big-time was setting in.

## TIME TO MOVE!

When God moved, things happened quickly. In Joshua 1:11, the next generation of Israelites had waited for forty years to possess the Promised Land. Suddenly God came to Joshua and said in three days, they were to cross the Jordan and possess the Land. Imagine having to pack up in three days and leave the desert…one would have thought that God would give them more time, like three months? But such is the nature of God. When God said, "Time to move!" it was decision time very quickly. He wanted us to move quickly to avoid paralysis due to too much analysis. No wonder I kept feeling the urgency to move on.

Things started falling in place at work as well. It was no coincidence that all my projects were coming to an end. In October 2010, I received news of another re-organization taking place in January 2011, the month that our office would be moving to the new place. In this new organization chart, I finally saw that I had no role left to play. The work I had been doing was complete and my old department was re-constituted. This meant that I might revert to doing what I had been doing for the past few years.

Around that time, I also found out that my bosses had recommended me for promotion to Deputy Director. Even though it did not materialize, I was really happy to hear that my capability was recognized and my bosses did think highly of me. God showed me that with this recognition; His restoration was complete. He wanted me to leave the past behind, for He was doing something new and better (Isa. 43:19).

When God began to do something new, it was usually hidden. He often kept it a secret until the last moment, because God liked to surprise us. In my humanness, I often envisioned how things would occur: like how I would conceive, give birth, then leave this organization. When it did not happen that way, I was initially confused and frustrated but I remembered God telling me that He would move me out of this place soon. I told myself I must be open to what God was doing to bring me out, even if it was different from what I expected. I was prepared to change when God was bringing the shift. I did not want to miss it, so I moved with Him.

Hence when He told me to resign even before I got pregnant, I was willing to obey. I was willing to stay home while waiting to become pregnant. After all, I had been asking for God to show me when I could resign since early 2010. Not only did God give me the green light to resign, He also told me there was urgency for me to leave this workplace and move on. I had to take the step of faith to resign now before I got pregnant. Even though I knew I would forego my performance bonus in April 2011 and my maternity benefits, I knew how important it was to obey the Lord and do it quickly when He called. He knew how things must be done even though I could not understand.

And so, I announced to my bosses that I would resign in December 2010 after my end-of-year bonus.

Of course, they tried to persuade me to stay till April for the performance bonus, but I refused. They even offered me part-time employment to let me stay, but I also turned them down. In the natural, it really seemed very silly to give up on the performance bonus. After all, I only had to stay three more months. God assured that even though I was giving up on my performance bonus in April 2011, He would not shortchange me in my finances. I had a sense that my husband would be promoted in January 2011 and he would receive a huge pay raise and fat bonuses. (It came to pass that he really got a huge pay raise and fat bonuses. Thank God for that!)

## God's Restoration Complete

It was amazing how the vision of me leaving this place with my head lifted up came to pass. During the last appraisal I had with my boss, she revealed that my highest potential was at Director Level. She said not many people have a potential that was as high. She felt that it was a pity that I decided to leave, for they could see that my career was taking off now. Even my human resource colleagues told me I was leaving at a high point of my career.

Eventually during my exit interview with my CEO, he told me that I was a leader. A leader was unlike a manager, for a leader had a vision, and he could motivate the rest to move toward that direction. My CEO said many people did not have the ability to join the dots and see the big picture, but I could. He would have been happy to see me stay, but he knew I had prayed about it for a while and he totally respected my decision.

> I never saw myself as a leader with a vision, but in recent years, God gave me a vision for my life. He caused me to see things in the future that others could not. This was from the wisdom of God; nothing that I could boast.

I really thank God for the spiritual vision He caused me to see and the leader He was molding me into.

With that, I finally left my workplace in January 2011, around the time when the office moved to the new place. I left the organization in peace and joy for I knew I had finished the race. I had finally completed my journey of waiting to leave this transitional place and God had caused me to close this chapter very well. Even though it had been almost three years (since I first had the strong desire to stay home in 2008) and it had not been an easy journey, God was with me every step of the way and He is faithful. What He had promised all came to pass. The vision eventually became reality. His Word proved to be true in the end.

The end of the season in my workplace also marked the beginning of my new season at home. In the short term, I knew I would be staying home, taking care of my children and being involved in my writing ministry. In the longer term, God might be leading me to something bigger that He had not revealed to me at this point. In any case, He had proven Himself to be trustworthy, and I was excited about my future because I knew that whatever God said would come to pass.

## Chapter 5

# MY NEW SEASON AT HOME

I OFFICIALLY STARTED MY season at home in February 2011. It was really so good…I remembered waking up in the morning but instead of rushing for work, I could spend a few hours reading the daily devotional, Bible, listening to sermons and fellowshiping with God. That first day at home marked the way I would be spending my future mornings in sweet fellowship with my Lord. With a steaming hot cup of coffee, I would then lounge comfortably into my red sofa in my bedroom, reading God's Word. Sometimes I would read the Bible, devotionals or Christian books, or I would listen to sermons and worship songs or spend an extended period in prayer, just talking and listening

47

to God. Other times I would break out into songs of praises, worshiping the Lord.

## SWEET FELLOWSHIP WITH GOD

My new home in this condo has a lovely environment. As we stayed on a low floor, I could see the beautiful landscape and the swimming pool. I felt like I lived in a garden—the Garden of Eden. Sometimes I would climb on the bay window to read my book and look at the residents walking by. There were a few occasions when I walked out to the river beside our condo. It was a park connector and there were people jogging in the morning. I would listen to a sermon or read a book when sitting by the river. Those were precious moments to me as I witnessed God's beautiful creation, like the trees dancing in the wind or the birds singing.

In the afternoons if Joshua took a nap, I would then blog about God's goodness or start writing the chapters of my book or typing my past journals into word documents. Sometimes I would cook dinner or do some housework. Other times I would bring Joshua out to the library or to swim, or host friends at my home. I told my husband that being able to spend so much time with the Lord was so luxurious. It was better than owning ten Louis Vuitton bags. I felt that I was already living in the Promised Land. Except for one thing—I was still waiting for the promise of my second child to come to pass.

# GOD'S GREATER PLANS

Even though I had the benefit of witnessing God's faithfulness in His promise of our first child, Joshua, I must say that the wait for this second baby was nevertheless not easy. Of course God was merciful and He never stopped encouraging me about how His promise was going to come to pass soon. However, deep in my heart there was still this longing desire that not only did not diminish…it intensified over time. I kept wondering, "God, You have already brought me to this stay-home season, what else are You waiting for? What is the delay?"

I thank God that I did not get confused or frustrated with God in the midst of waiting. In any case, I was enjoying the abundant life that Jesus came to give us. I really did not have anything to complain about—I had no work stress, I was no longer in a narrow place, and I was enjoying unhindered fellowship and intimacy with my Lord. Out of the overflow of the abundance in my heart, the Lord caused me to minister to many sisters even while I stayed home. I was able to encourage them with the Word of God either through meeting up with them or a phone call or an email message. God is so good. He enabled me to be involved in ministry work even while I stayed at home taking care of Joshua.

As I pressed in to seek the Lord more regarding His timing of another child, the Lord revealed many wonderful things to me. He showed me that from the start, this faith lesson was never just about the timing issue of another child. He had greater issues at stake than the specific prayer that I brought to Him. As I learned to let go of this perennial timing issue that held me in bondage for years, He slowly revealed His plan for me. I was astounded to find out that it had to do with my future ministry and my divine destiny.

And as I retraced the journey God had walked with me over the past four years waiting for this child, I saw more of His good intentions for me. I also understood that even when God moved me into this season of childbearing in February 2011, the process and fight of faith was not finished. There was still a persevering that needed to happen. There was still some pushing if the fullness stage of birth was to be reached. Yet the end result was always worth the pain and the discomfort.

Victory might be very, very close but often that was when the battle became more intense. I learned that one of my divine destinies was to give birth to champions in God's kingdom.

> Destiny was always contested and the evil one would put up a fight to prevent us from fulfilling that destiny.

He would try to keep us from experiencing the breakthroughs God wanted us to have and for which we have been believing (in our case, our second baby). We were guaranteed success when we have fought the good fight of faith, which would bring us abundant spoils. When I saw that, I understood why the delay.

It was in hindsight that I realized He was preparing me for my future ministry. God was training me, preparing me and renewing my mind for His future assignments. The new levels of fruitfulness require new levels of knowledge, insight, and faith. Often the insight I received from the waiting season was actually meant to help me in the future stages God is bringing me to.

When I was progressing with God, moving forward as He trusted me with more, He constantly stretched me. I could not say that it was pleasant, but the end result was that it produced in me the peaceable fruit of righteousness to those who have been trained by it (Heb. 12:11). God also brought me to a higher level of faith because the faith He required from me in my future was not the same as yesterday.

## TEACHING ON RIGHTEOUSNESS REVISITED

I always thought I knew the teaching on righteousness very well. After all, we were well taught by Pastor Prince. However, God brought this teaching to my mind again as I was reading Pastor Prince's devotional on the righteousness of God.

---

Righteousness is right believing
in the finished work of Jesus
Christ and it is not right doing.

---

Hence we cannot be more righteous just as we cannot be "more saved." Pastor Prince always says, "Right believing leads to right doing," so we can be sure when we believe right, we will always do things the way God wanted.

It was so important while waiting for our miracle, when we lapsed into thinking there was something wrong with us, that we knew how to respond to such accusing voices. When we were established in righteousness, we know it was not about us or our efforts. It was a finished work of Christ at the Cross. We know that whether we do anything or nothing about our situation, it will not affect the manifestation. What we believe in, not what we do, is more important to receiving God's miracle.

God also taught me that once my heart is established in righteousness in Christ, I cannot be persuaded by the devil to believe that he can enforce bad things in my life. This is how I resist the devil—by standing steadfast in the faith (1 Pet. 5:9) that I am made right with God by Jesus' blood. This pregnancy would come to pass whether I did anything about it at all. My self-efforts may fail but Christ cannot fail. Once I am established in righteousness, I shall be far from oppression, I shall not fear; and from terror, for it shall not come near me (Isa. 54:14).

You may wonder what the righteousness of God has to do with receiving this child. I can tell you that the righteousness of God has everything to do with this!

Understanding and believing that we are the righteousness of God is the key to receiving all the blessings in this life.

> Pastor Prince always says law is natural but grace is not. It is human nature to lapse back to the law (self-efforts) and the natural. Hence we always have to keep hearing the gospel of grace.

We need to know that the price has been paid by Jesus and His promise is sure. As God's people, we walk by faith not by sight, so even if the promise has not yet manifested in the natural, we choose to focus on Christ rather than on the circumstances.

## REJOICE AND CELEBRATE!

In the process of waiting, God also taught me about His great love for me and my husband's love for me. In response, I was motivated to love Jesus more and enjoy my lord (husband) in the process of intimacy, instead of focusing on the outcome—the baby. God wanted me to enjoy the entire process, rest in Him, and leave the result to Him. He wanted this baby to be conceived in the midst of rest and joy, not self-efforts or worry. He wanted me to celebrate our love and our marriage. God is really so good—He has my best interests at heart.

I remember telling God that it would be easy for

Him to make me pregnant, but I hoped this second pregnancy would bring Him more glory than my first pregnancy. I told Him that it was more important for me to pass the faith test, to finish the race and close this chapter of waiting well. In fact, God said He was pleased that I had passed the faith test with flying colors and I had closed each chapter of my life in the past four years well.

Then from July 2011, God started to tell me to rejoice and celebrate for the marvelous things He has done in my life. I knew one of them would be the manifestation of my baby. I was happy and excited to hear this. I remember the last time He had told me to celebrate, in July 2010, things quickly fell into place in my workplace; and by September 2010, God had given me the instruction to quit my organization.

Not only that, God also showed me Isaiah 42:9, "Behold, the former things have come to pass, and new things I declare; before they spring forth I tell you of them," and Isaiah 43:19, "Behold, I will do a new thing, now it shall spring forth; shall you not know it?" I knew these were verses connoting God's divine shifts. God was telling me He was doing something new. Now it springs forth. The former things have come to pass and the new thing is happening. He was slowly revealing to me new things He was doing in my future ministry. You know, when God speaks, He will keep bombarding you with the same messages—and I loved it! I loved to hear Him speak nonstop to me.

# REMEMBER THE LORD

At one point God led me to retrace the journey He had walked with me over the past four years. His key objective was to tell me to remember it was the Lord who brought me through the desert to test me and to humble me (Deut. 8:2). He wanted me to always remember it was He who gave us the power to obtain wealth so that when we were very prosperous, we would not say it was our own hands that made us so (Deut. 8:17–18). He showed me that the journey of faith was necessary so that I would learn to rely on nothing but the Word of God (Deut. 8:3), because He was about to bring me into the Promised Land: a place flowing with milk and honey.

God also told me to set up memorial stones to commemorate this journey so that my future descendants would know of His faithfulness and the miracles He has performed in our lives. At this, I was reminded of setting up memorial stones in 2005 because God was leading me into the Promised Land, just before I conceived Joshua. I was really touched by this, because it was always me asking God to remember me. Now it was the other way around.

God really has my best interests at heart. He knew that once I was in the Promised Land, I could easily forget Him, like the Israelites did. Hence He had to keep reminding me to keep His Word in my heart like He did in 2005 with the verse Joshua 1:8, "This Book of the Law shall not depart from your mouth, but you shall meditate in it day and night, that you may observe to do according to all that is written in it." And so, the memorial stones I set up were to document all the journals I had written over the years so that they could in turn be published into books to bless many others.

## Now Is the Time!

God also showed me that none of His words would be delayed any longer, it shall be done (Ezek. 12:28), and that He is changing the times and seasons (Dan. 2:21). These verses told me that He was bringing me into the fullness stage when He would reveal this baby, this pregnancy to me. He kept telling me that whatever He said would come to pass and every vision would be fulfilled in spite of the contrary natural circumstances.

In September 2011, God encouraged me with Habakkuk 2:3 that there was indeed an appointed time for this vision to be fulfilled and it spoke of the end. After this verse I kept seeing "the end" like in Ecclesiastes 7:8, "The end of a matter is better than its beginning." Everywhere I turned God seemed to be telling me that the end was here. I had finally reached the finish line and the long wait had finally ended. This pregnancy was coming to pass soon.

So I boldly declared, "My time is coming…God is working behind the scenes on my behalf. He will fulfill the plan He has for me." I reminded myself of God's faithfulness and if I did what He said (to celebrate before I see the manifestation), He would do what He said. After all, the battle belonged to the Lord. All I had to do was cooperate with God, stand in faith, and stay in position. I needed to stir up my faith to believe that God can rapidly orchestrate the changes. God is so good. He provided me with the second wind to give the final push to see this "baby" delivered. He granted me strength to push past the discomfort and pain of contractions to delivery.

As I humbled myself and asked for my care group members to stand in faith with us on this promise, God also sent encouragement through brothers and sisters in Christ (and even Joshua) who told us about their dreams and visions of me having a baby girl. My dear brothers in care group also assured me that our baby was on the way soon and we were next! Well, God's confirmation was a resounding yes! Therefore I was reminded of Hebrews 12:1–2, that since I am surrounded by such a great crowd of witnesses, I shall throw off anything that hinders and run the race with endurance, fixing my eyes on Jesus, the author and perfector of my faith!

## FULFILLMENT OF GOD'S PROMISE OF A SECOND CHILD

In the beginning of 2011, Pastor Prince told our church to bring our three requests to God and he prayed over them. He said there was something special about bringing our requests to God in a church, for there was a corporate anointing. He prophesied that 2011 was the year of God's crowned goodness and our paths drip with abundance (Ps. 65:11). He also said that it was a year of fertility for those who desired to have a baby.

Indeed in the course of the year, many ladies got pregnant because they asked God for it. Even Pastor's wife conceived. As I was still waiting to see the fulfillment of God's promise in this area of my life, I kept telling myself that I, too, sat under the corporate anointing. I was there together with the other ladies. One of my three wishes was to have my second baby in this year. I knew God is no respecter of men and that I would not be left out.

Towards the last month of 2011, I was still anticipating this piece of good news. The excitement was heightened because of God's word to me, confirming this pregnancy; that I have truly conceived. Yet instead of seeing the manifestation, I experienced great spiritual resistance through some senseless gum pains. It took me a week to recover. All these happened before the turn of 2012. The devil robbed me of the joy in celebrating Christmas and New Year. But I know my Lord will cause him to repay double what he stole from me.

Deep down I knew that the spiritual attack was the devil's last desperate shot. God had prepared something very good for me in 2012 and He was just waiting for me to cross over to the New Year. I believed God was about to reveal to me this pregnancy, and that when I found out about it, I would be two months pregnant. It would be a supernatural conception because God caused me to conceive despite menstruation. He is the Lord over the natural circumstances. I would not know how this was possible, but with God, everything is possible. All I would know was that the power of the Most High God came upon me and overshadowed me.

True enough, as the Lord has shown me, I conceived in early 2012. One fine day I woke up and was prompted by the Holy Spirit to take a pregnancy test. I could not remember how many times I had taken pregnancy tests and the results were all negative. But yet this day I had the peace to take the test again. I knew in my heart I had conceived because of what the Lord has said. This quiet assurance was definitely from the Lord and not the natural circumstances. I prayed in tongues as I waited for the test results. My heart was still beating very fast as I picked up the test kit. Praise the Lord! There were two lines, meaning that I had conceived! I have replayed this scene almost a thousand times in my mind but nothing beats the real thing! My tears were tears of joy because of the fulfillment of God's promise despite the four years of waiting. God is really so good to me!

**Chapter 6**

# THROUGH IT ALL

A REVIEW OF MY life journey for the past decade drew precious lessons for me. As God brought me through each season of my life, I realized that He was doing different things at different stages. He put me through processes of change so that He could pour out more of His Spirit unto us and prepare us for the new season. Change was the only constant in our Christian walk. He renewed our minds in the sense that He radically transformed the way we think so that we could participate in the new thing He was doing.

## RENEWING OF OUR MINDS

The renewal process was usually in two stages: quantitatively renewed and qualitatively renewed. In the first stage, God restored us back to something we had before. In my case, it was a restoration of the child that the devil had stolen and the honor that I had lost in the first reorganization. God's work also involved a restoration of my trust in Him, my first love for Him, and a return to the level of faith in which I previously walked with Him.

The second stage of qualitative renewal was when God brought about another stage of newness, and the end result was that we were different from before. This process was more than just restoration; it was a transformation into the image of Christ. Rather than just restoring us to where we were, He renewed us to a fresh new place. When He was finished with the work He started in us, we would not look or feel the same. We were ready for a shift to more outpouring of His Spirit. Planting us in NCC and saturating us with the gospel of grace was God's way to bring about this new mind-set in us. As I got to know more about Jesus, my lovely Savior, I realized that I was slowly being transformed into the glory of my Lord (2 Cor. 3:18).

In Joel 2:25, God says, "So I will restore to you the years that the swarming locust has eaten," and in Joel 2:28, God says, "And it shall come to pass afterward that I will pour out My Spirit on all flesh; your sons and daughters shall prophesy, your old men shall dream dreams, your young men shall see visions." What God was saying here was that before He poured out more of His Spirit on us, He would restore to us the years the devil has stolen.

---

## So you see, restoration always comes before the outpouring of His Spirit, which results in a great work of God.

---

When God takes us to new levels of growth, we are often very shortsighted about it. We think it is simply to bless us or reward our faithfulness; when in reality, it is often to bless others. God usually has greater issues at stake when we come to Him with the specific prayer we have on hand. Like for me, when I kept going to God about the timing issue of my second child, He showed me that it was not just about this promised child. Unless God renewed our mind, we would not be able to accept the greater plans He has for us. In my case, God was not just preparing me to receive this child, but He was also training me for my future ministry. Besides, He showed me that my ministry would be far greater than what I can ask or imagine (Eph. 3:20).

## WAITING ON GOD

As I looked back at the journey, I must say that it has been difficult at times. However, I knew deep down there was peace and joy, knowing that I was living in the center of God's will. God has also proven once and again that for those who waited faithfully for His promises to be fulfilled, their day would come. For me, the day came to start my stay-home season, which had been my heart's desire for the past three years. God's timing was sure and He never disappointed me in the end.

Waiting for God could be tough, as many discouragements and distractions, even confusion, worked to pull our eyes away from what the Lord had promised us. After waiting for a long while, I even started questioning whether this was really His will or whether I heard Him correctly. I doubted my ability to hear from God, when Jesus clearly said, "My sheep listen to my voice" (John 10:27, NIV). I could understand why people get bitter and angry with God, because they felt God's timing moved too slowly for them. It could be painful when the thing you have been waiting for did not materialize day after day, month after month, and year after year.

For me, I came to a point when I was prepared to compromise, to settle for God's second best. I was willing to trade God's provision for my stay-home days in return for a faster fulfillment of His promise of my second child. How silly I am, right? That was because I never realized that my passing of the faith test would impact my future generation. I had the privilege of starting a new ripple effect of blessing for future generations, which of course I could not see then. I was focusing on the short-term while God was looking at the longer range.

I came to learn that confusion during the waiting period was normal. There were many times in my journey when I was perplexed by the situations that did not go the way I expected. When circumstances went contrary to the Word of God, I was so tempted to ask, "This doesn't make sense. I have put my faith in Jesus. I am a child of the Most High God. Why is this happening? God, what are You doing?" At that point in time, God did not reveal His purpose or His timing. He knew I was not in a state of mind for answers. He just kept telling me that my season was changing and gave me strength to carry on with the race. But now, I learned that the circumstances do not change God's Word. On the contrary, God's Word has the power to change the circumstances.

## BENEFITS OF TOUGH TIMES

While reading the book, *You Were Made for More* by Jim Cymbala,[1] I really can understand what he meant when he talked about going through tough times. He talked about how such challenges and difficulties produce a number of benefits in our lives. I could apply what he had taught to my specific situation.

Firstly, he said such hardships produce iron in our souls. These experiences cause new kinds of growth, producing tenacity and endurance. In the process of waiting, I thought I was doing what I should, but God was still not coming through for me (or at least I thought). Other times I would condemn myself for doubting God's promise or that my faith was not high enough. Either way it was painful because the focus was on self. But now I know that such tough times are indicators that God is preparing me for something special down the road. God is honing my spiritual muscles through these resistances in my life; He is building my spiritual growth.

> What kept me going on despite the confusion and frustration was that God loves me more than I can imagine and that He is a good God.

Secondly, he taught that these difficult times give birth to the practice of prayer on a whole new level. I called out to God so many times like never before. I was so desperate for God to answer me: when is my next season coming, why is it not happening yet, why the delay? The sense of weakness (that I was totally helpless) was what brought me to the throne of grace in times of need. These are like catalysts that brought me closer to God. Once when I was so disappointed, I told God I did not even want an answer for the delay, I just want Jesus. I finally came to a point when I esteemed Jesus far above the things I desired or even God's promises for my life. These blessings of God are precious to me but they can never take the place of my Lord Jesus, the Blesser.

Thirdly, such hardships give us a story to tell. God told me to create memorial stones out of this experience of waiting for His promises, to make sure my children catch the importance of this journey. It was all about God's miraculous power in my life and His faithfulness to me at times when I did not know where to turn. One day my testimony would be even made known to the nations through my publications. In the future, someone who is going through difficult times will be inspired and encouraged by my story, just like how the Exodus story inspires the Jews even today. God knew that His people may not always relate to His Word but similar experiences always serve to connect and encourage. God must have allowed such experiences in my life for a good purpose.

## ALL ABOUT GOD

Eventually I learned that what God does in my life is not just about me, myself, and I. He is doing things that will overflow to the lives of others through our testimonies of His faithfulness. Through these testimonies, the victories of the past will be put to strategic use in the future. In the final analysis, I learned that everything in my life is really about God and His Son, Jesus. Hence all glory belongs to God!

# NOTES

### CHAPTER 1: MY JOURNEY WITH FAITH TEACHINGS

1.  Kenneth E. Hagin, Don't Blame God (Tulsa, OK: Faith Library Publications, 1979).

2.  Francis MacNutt and Judith MacNutt, Praying for Your Unborn Child (London: Hodder & Stoughton Ltd, 1988).

### CHAPTER 4: CALLING OUT OF MY OLD WORKPLACE

1.  Joel Osteen, It's Your Time: Activate Your Faith, Achieve Your Dreams, and Increase in God's Favor (New York: Free Press, 2009).

### CHAPTER 6: THROUGH IT ALL

1.  Jim Cymbala, You Were Made for More (Grand Rapids, MI: Zondervan, 2008).

# ABOUT THE AUTHOR

AVIN LEE GRADUATED with a business degree from a university in Singapore. She worked in the government sector for about fifteen years. However, in 2008, she sensed that God was calling her to be a full-time stay-home mum. She eventually quit her job in January 2011. Her passion is to see young mothers grow in their relationship with Christ and to celebrate their lives as beautiful individuals with divine destinies. She is happily married to Heng with a six-year-old son, Joshua. The family currently attends New Creation Church pastored by Joseph Prince in Singapore. She is now serving as a care group leader in church.

# CONTACT THE AUTHOR

You are welcome to e-mail your comments to the author at:

avinlee77@gmail. com